AGRIGENTO

THE VALLEY OF THE TEMPLES AND SURROUNDINGS

LORETTA SANTINI

CENTRO STAMPA EDITORIALE
plurigraf
PERSEUS

Agrigento: the fascination of the past

".... The other evening, when we were in sight of Akragas, the sun was setting, transfiguring the columns of these simple but harmoniously proportioned structures, as if a whole luminosity of stone were being emitted from them. Nowhere in Greece proper, with the exception of the Parthenon, does one succeed in having such an evocation of the Hellenic world."

With these words Bernard Berenson re-evoked, in the account he wrote of his journey to Sicily, the magic and incomparable spectacle presented to his eyes by the Valley of the Temples of Agrigento. In fact this exceptional archaeological heritage scattered over the valley below the town is one which has no equal other than on Greek soil itself. It bears eloquent witness to the extraordinary historical event which led the inhabitants of ancient Greece to cross the seas and establish numerous colonies along the whole coast of southern Italy. These, under the impulse of the mother country, often achieved an equal level of civilization and of artistic and social development.

A real cultural revolution was determined following colonization, and this extraordinary revolu-tion also made its effects felt on Agrigento, which became one of the most magnificent cities of Magna Graecia, as is demonstrated by the exceptional nature of the archaeological finds and the artistic level to which they testify.

ORIGINS

Even though the first traces of human life in Agrigentine territory date back to the prehistoric period (the most numerous finds date to the Bronze Age and are especially concentrated in the locality of Serraferlicchio), the city of Agrigento itself was officially founded by Rhodian colonists from Gela in 581 BC. It was therefore initially a sub-colony of Greece. Its founders gave it the name of Akragas, from the river of the same name which runs in its vicinity.

It requires no ingenuity to suppose that the choice of the site was determined by environmental reasons: the presence of rivers (the Akragas and the Hypsas) ensured the fertility of the soil, while a naturally fortified rocky escarpment - on which the Acropolis was to arise - ensured its defence from any hostile attacks.

A number of legends are associated with the history of the city's foundation. According to one of these, the city was founded at the behest of Acragantes, son of Zeus, and a nymph. Another relates that it was founded by Daedalus who, on flying over Sicily with the wings he himself had made, to escape from the labyrinth of the Minotaur, saw the site of the town and fell in love with it.

HISTORY

Akragas initially shared the constitutional and legal system of Gela, its mother country.

The first tyrant of the city was Phalaris, who began to extend Agrigentine dominion over the surrounding peoples and to build up the future power of Akragas.

Under Theron, the second tyrant (488-473 BC), the city's importance grew and its domination over the surrounding territories extended as far as Himera.

He also began to fortify the site and to organize the city's internal layout: a long circuit of wall was built around the city, reinforced at its weakest points with square towers and equipped with numerous gates. Streets were laid out, and an elaborate drainage system developed.

The political and military power of Akragas reached its zenith under Theron and more especially after the victory over the Carthaginians at Himera (480 BC), putting a end for the moment to their expansionist goals in Sicily and southern Italy.

It was then that Agrigento reached the zenith of its wealth and power.

The city was hailed by the Greek poet Pindar as "of incredible opulence" and "the most beautiful city of mortals".

This period was also characterized by a building boom which led to the realization of the magnificent ensemble of works of art which constitutes the Valley of the Temples, also with the aim of emulating the great models of Greek Doric architecture. In the space of just a few years no less than nine new temples were erected. One of them, that of Olympian Zeus, was of such enormous dimensions as to be considered the third largest temple of antiquity.

It was also during this period, which we could call the golden age of Akragas, that the great philosopher Empedocles lived and worked in the city. It was to this city that thinkers, poets and sculptors of great talent, such as Pindar, Pythagoras, Miron and Zeuxis, flocked from Greece. All the arts were cultivated and fostered, and the city basked in its fame and its luxury.

This was followed by a period of vicissitudes. Having remained neutral in the war between Athens and Syracuse, the great city of Akragas failed to fight off the assault of the Carthaginians, who in 406 BC, after a siege of eight months, finally captured her, plundered her and put her to the flame. Agrigento then lost its territories and a large part of its importance.

It revived several years later, especially thanks to the efforts of Timoleon, who defeated the Carthaginians in battle in 340. The city then reconquered part of its former splendor and experienced a new period of urban expansion which we can

now identify in the remains of what is called the Hellenistic-Roman quarter of the city.

During the Punic wars, Akragas allied itself now with Carthage, now with Rome, and was subjected to renewed sacking, devastation and fire, until it was finally occupied by the Romans in 210 AD. The Romans changed its name, giving it the new name of Agrigentum.

Under Roman rule, the city enjoyed a long period of economic prosperity (it always remained a major mercantile and agricultural centre), relative peace and further urban expansion.

The decline of the city, which even in the last centuries of the Roman Republic was still recorded as one of the most important cities in Sicily, began in an irreversible way during the imperial period. Sicily, and Agrigento in particular, were progressively removed from the frontiers of Rome which had now expanded well beyond the geographical confines of Italy; excluded from the major trade routes of the Roman world, they were displaced from the centre of economic and political life.

Subsequently Agrigento suffered the tragedy of the barbarian invasions: Vandals and Goths alternated for over a century in their destructive raids on Sicily, sacking and destroying everything they encountered on their path.

Absorbed into the Byzantine Empire, the city never regained its ancient splendor.

In 827 it was occupied by the Arabs who changed its ancient name to Girgenti ("Gergent"). Under Arab rule, the city once again enjoyed a favorable period: the economy, and in particular, trade, was developed, its population increased, and it underwent a new urbanistic impulse which took the form especially of the transformation of the quarters of the historic city centre according to the style and characteristics of Islamic towns (blind alleys, overhead arches, winding streets, inner courtyards, passages and links between the various houses).

In 1087 it was conquered by the Normans and subsequently· became an important episcopal see and regional capi-

tal.

Between the end of the 13th century and the first half of the 14th it was a fief of the Chiaromonte family, perhaps the most powerful in Sicily at the time.

Under successive Aragonese and Spanish rule it maintained a certain importance and prestige, and various privileges were conferred on it, such as that of customs exemption which favored it in the mercantile field.

In the modern period, in spite of the fact that it was one of the cities least oppressed by Bourbon maladministration, after Garibaldi had raised his standard at Salemi on 14 May 1860, Girgenti and all the municipalities of the province rose against the Bourbons, and took an active part in the wars for independence and the unification of Italy.

A GLANCE AT THE MODERN CITY

Agrigento, a name derived from its ancient Latin name which the city resumed only in 1927, now stands in a truly magnificent position, overlooking the Valley of the Temples and with views of the sea.

It occupies the acropolis of ancient Akragas, and is spread over the southern slopes of two contiguous hills.

In the irregular structure of its winding and precipitous alleyways, in the narrow crowded spaces of the old urban fabric, in the buildings and monuments facing onto the very central Via Atenea, the city preserves many traces and aspects of its medieval and baroque past.

The Cathedral; the Cathedral Museum containing some really wonderful works of art; the church of Santa Maria dei Greci; the Palazzo del Seminario; the Monastery of Santo Spirito; and the church of San Nicola with its modern Regional Archeological Museum, are just some of the finest monuments in the city.

But what really constitutes the glory of Agrigento, and attracts visitors from all over the world, is without doubt the Valley of the Temples, which bears incomparable testimony to the splendor and perfection which Doric art attained in the Greek colonies of southern Italy and Sicily.

Akragas and the Valley of the Temples: the Ancient City

It was only after the Second World War that systematic excavations began on the site. These have brought to light very ancient and important ruins, ranging in date from the prehistoric period to the late Christian era, and achieving their culmination in the Greek temples.

Of the latter, the largest is the Temple of Olympian Zeus. It was built from 480 BC on, after the victory at Himera, and with the use of large numbers of Carthaginian prisoners. Its construction, according to the reports of several writers, was apparently never completed.

The most ancient of the Agrigentine temples is the Temple of Hercules: it dates back to the late 6th century BC and now consists of no more than eight surviving columns, of which four, are complete with their capitals.

The most beautiful of the temples of ancient Agrigento was probably the so-called Temple of Concord, which dates to the late 6th century BC. However it is not known to which god it was dedicated.

Only four columns supporting a fragment of pediment remain of the Temple of Castor and Pollux, but due to their harmonious and elegant composition they have become the emblem of Agrigento.

The Temple of Juno is very large. Of its thirty-four original columns, twenty-five are still standing, some of them supporting the architrave.

Adjacent to the temples some important remains have been revealed by the excavations: ranging from the cemeteries of rock-cut tombs of the prehistoric period to the so-called tomb of Theron dating to the initial period of Roman rule, and the Christian catacombs.

A Glance at the Area of Agrigento

Apart from the historic city center and the splendor of the Doric temples, Agrigento also possesses many natural beauties: the almost perennial serenity of the sky, the spring-like balminess of the climate. The unspoiled fascination of the coastline, the poetic beauty of the almond-trees in flower, whose period of blossom each year is accompanied by a picturesque Festival during which folkloristic groups from all over the world celebrate the return of spring, in a scenic setting rich in color and music, and raise a hymn of brotherhood among peoples.

Then there are the environs of Agrigento: Sciacca an ancient Greek colony; Licata, a town rich in history; Porto Empedocle, a maritime and industrial city.

Lastly the islands: Linosa, Lampedusa, Lampione, where the fascination of a wild and uncontaminated natural environment is still preserved intact. The coastline of these islands is spell-binding: cliffs dropping sheer to a crystal-clear, unpolluted sea; huge caves in which the water assumes the most varied and delicate colorations; and little bays and inlets of the finest golden sand.

All these natural beauties, together with the enormous archaeological heritage, make Agrigento and its environs an agreeable vacation centre and a compulsory goal for any tourist visiting Sicily.

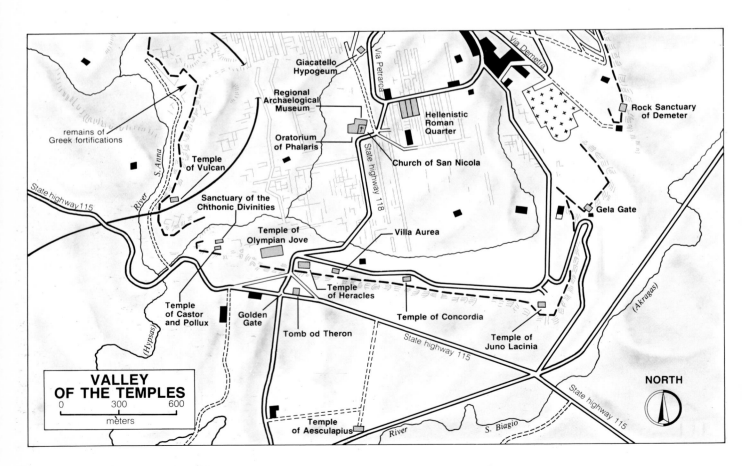

Temple of Olympian Zeus

The temple is dedicated to Zeus, father of all the gods and lord of Olympus. For this reason it is also known as the "Olympieion". It survives as a gigantic scatter of ruins, which immediately suggests that it must have been of colossal dimensions. In fact it measured some 113 metres in length and 56.30 in width. In spite of the fact that only the structures of the podium and a few other architectural elements remain visible to this day, the impression one gets from these ruins is one of imposing grandeur and awesome monumentality. Indeed, in terms of mere size, it was the third biggest religious building of antiquity. Erected between 480 and 470 BC, immediately after the victory of Himera - a victory that marked the period of maximum splendor of ancient Agrigento - the temple represents, in architectural terms, an undoubtedly innovative experience. This is apparent not only as regards the building's structural form (it is in fact a pseudo- peripteral termple, which means that its exterior colonnading did not follow, as was usual in this type of sanctuary, the whole perimeter of the temple; instead, the columns along one side of the building were replaced by a wall articulated by engaged half-columns. But the temple is also innovative for its method of construction, for example the practice of deriving some elements of the building from a single block of material in order to facilitate their putting into place. Yet the most striking feature of the Temple of Zeus are its colossal "TELAMONES": the huge caryatids or columns in the form of a male figure, which were used to support the entablature. They are some 8 metres in height (one is preserved in the Regional Archaeological Museum, while a copy of it can be seen recumbent on the ground by the Temple in all its length). These figures represent an extraordinary testimony to the creativeness of the architects of the temple. They also attest to their ability to devise original architectural solutions aimed at increasing the stability of the building which, in view of its exceptional size, might otherwise have posed problems of static equilibrium. These enormous figures were in fact incorporated in

General view of the remains of the Temple of Zeus. The layout of the sanctuary is easily recognisable.

the interspace between the columns and served to support the lateral entablatures. The interior of the Temple of Zeus consisted of a double row of pillars which divided it into three aisles. The cella, or inner sanctuary of the god, was also tripartite in structure. The decorations of the Sactuary, unfortunately now lost, included - as we are told by the ancient historians - a pedimental sculptural representation of the "Battle of the Giants" and the "Trojan War". These were all reliefs of colossal size and hence in line with the exceptional size of the building as a whole.

One of the large capitals that once crowned the columns arises out of the ruins of the Temple of Jupiter (Giove olimpico).

Below, one of the immense Telemons that decorated the temple; the reconstructed cast of one is visible on the ground; the original was removed and reassembled in the Archaeological Museum.

Temple of Chthonian Gods

The monumental complex to which this name is attached is not so much a temple proper as a series of buildings, in a particular archaeological sector of the Valley of the Temples (in proximity of Gate V of the city). This is a sector which presents architectural features, styles and complexes of various kind, structure and function, dating to different periods, but all sharing the common denominator of fulfilling a sacred function. The complex consists of a group of small and large religious buildings, shrines and altars, erected roughly between the 7th and 6th century BC, and mainly dedicated to the goddesses Demeter and Kore (or Persephone), protectresses of the earth and hence known as "chthonic deities", meaning terrestial deities. Some of these sanctuaries may even be considered as predating the foundation of the city and hence linked essentially to primitive local cults. The sacred complex originally took the form of two archaic *temenoi* (i.e. sacred enclosures) which enclose a series of altars either rectangular in plan or circular and in several cases monolithic, recalling the form of a well and perhaps connected with a primitive cult of water. To these primitive altars were added, in subsequent periods, some small temples, also furnished with pronaos and cella (inner sanctuary) for the god, which enriched the sacred area. The archaeological complex was excavated in the first two decades of the present century by Pirro Marconi, who also conducted the studies relating to the sacred enclosures of Akragas.

In the foreground, a circular altar in the sanctuary of the Chthonian Gods; in the background are the ruins of the Temple of Castor and Pollux.

Temple of Castor and Pollux

The Temple of Castor and Pollux or of the Dioscuri (they were the sons of Zeus) offers a suggestive image of 4 corner columns surmounted by an elegant trabeation and what remains of the pronounced pediment. The remains of the temple are situated on the edge of the sacred area known as the Sanctuary of the Chthonian Deities and form an integral part of it.

The temple was undoubtedly erected in the 5th century BC, but was soon afterwards damaged following the destruction caused by the invading Carthaginians.

The elegant trabeation which now surmounts the colonnade probably dates to a reconstruction of the building in the Hellenistic period. It was probably a peripteral and hexastyle temple (i.e. with six columns in front).

This page and right, a view of the surviving columns of the Dioscuri Temple. Just visible are the remains of a plaster decoration.

Following pages, a view of the sanctuary of the Chthonian Gods and Temple of Castor and Pollux; another view of the temple.

Temple of Hercules

The temple, with all its archaic fascination, is situated in the furthermost stretch of the Via dei Templi. Its tall columns, in part surmounted by flat capitals, are aligned in rhythmic succession along the side of the Sanctuary, rising over a podium approached by three high stone steps. The notable length of this temple, the massiveness of its columns and the structure of its capitals, are all stylistic features dating it to the late 6th century, that is, to a period preceding that of the other sacred buildings of the Valley of the Temples. It too is a peripteron (i.e. with the colonnade distributed right round its external perimeter) and hexastyle (i.e. with six columns on its shorter sides). It is ascribable to the golden period of Greek archaic architecture, of which its massive and well-balanced architectural structure is indeed one of the finest expressions. The temple is dedicated to Hercules, a Greek mythological figure, man and god at the same time. A bronze statue of Hercules embellished the temple. It is mentioned in the ancient sources by Livy and Cicero, both of whom confirm its beauty and the fact that it was the object of a lively cult by the local population. Cicero recalls in his orations against Verres that the latter, at the time of his governorship in the island, had tried to gain possession of it.

Left, a fascinating view of the area where the Temple of Castor and Pollux stands.

This page, a detail of the Temple of Hercules.

Following pages, two views of the temple. Standing out among the many ruins, and raised in 1924, are eight columns of the 44 that originally decorated the building.

Tomb of Theron

This is a so-called *heroon*, a monumental tomb incorporated in the extensive suburban area of the city's burial grounds-, in other words in the territory which extends beyond the circuit of walls of ancient Akragas in the vicinity of the Porta Aurea. The *heroon* is a sepulchral building which was traditionally dedicated to the heroes who were glorified by the ancient Greeks and given equal status to the gods.

The monument, however, dates to the Roman period (like others in the necropolis of which only the basements remain). Hence it is not to be considered a tomb raised in honor of the historical Theron, who was the Agrigentine tyrant responsible for the victory at Himera and lord of Agrigento during its most splendid period in the 5th century BC. The monument, which is probably incomplete because it lacks its upper part which almost certainly ended in a point or pinnacle, consists of a solid rectangular basement built of squared blocks of marble. It is marked by a pronounced cornice in the Hellenistic style, above which rises the tomb itself, also cubic in shape. This upper part of the monument is characterized by the handsome corner columns incorporated into the wall structure and by blind doors. The architectural complex has essentially the structure of a tower with a base that is wider than its superstructure and hence with a slightly pyramidal shape.

In the southernmost area of the site is the Tomb of Theron, set amidst particularly attractive scenery. In the background are the ruins of the Temple of Hercules.

Temple of Aesculapius

The Temple of Aesculapius, whose remains were brought to light in 1926, is situated on the banks of the river Akragas, in the plain sloping down to the sea to the south of the Valley of the Temples. It is a small temple *in antis* (i.e. with a rectangular structure with two frontal columns) with pseudoportico, perhaps dating to the 5th century BC. It contained the famous statue of Apollo, a work of Myron, plundered by the Carthaginian Himilco, recovered by Scipio and then stolen by Verres.

Early Christian Cemetery

Ancient Agrigento, which had enjoyed such fame under the Greeks as attested by the splendid monuments which today make it one of the most interesting and fascinating archaeological zones in the world, maintained a large part of its importance and prosperity also under the Romans down to the imperial period. With the fall of the Empire, the city, like a large part of the region's territory, underwent a considerable economic, social and political decline. With the spread of Christianity in Sicily, numerous cemeteries came to be situated in this zone. Of some importance are the tombs in the eastern part of the hill of the Temples in the environs of the Temple of Concord. They belong to Byzantine-Christian burial grounds largely dating to the 4th and 5th centuries AD. Some of these tombs are particularly striking because they are hewn into the rock and connected by underground corridors typical of many catacombs.

The Temple of Aesculapius with the Temple of Concordia in the background.

Right, the remains of the early Christian necropolis.

Temple of Concord

We are here confronted by one of the largest and best preserved monuments of antiquity. Its superb ruins rise along the crest of the hill of the Temples and constitute an exceptional example of the Doric style in its most harmonious and well-proportioned form.

The monument undoubtedly represents one of the most significant achievements of Greek architecture, thanks to the perfection and equilibrium it achieves in the modelling and fusion of its structural elements and to its skilful application of the canons of the Doric style.

The temple was built in the 5th century BC.

We have no contemporary sources to tell us after which Greek deity it was named. It was however dedicated to "Concord" in the 16th century: a name that was derived from the words of an inscription found in its vicinity.

The building is a peripteron (with the columns placed right round its perimeter) and with 6 columns on its shorter sides. It rises over a podium raised over four steps.

The columns are surmounted by Doric capitals. They in turn support a long architrave which runs along the sanctuary's perimeter. Above that in turn was the pediment and the ridged roof (which has collapsed and is no longer visible).

Inside the temple was the cella of the god, which was raised in height over the podium.

Originally the temple was embellished with magnificent stucco decoration, which gave the optical effect of marble revetment.

An impressive view of the façade of the Temple of Concordia.

Following pages, various views of the temple, built in the 5th century B.C.

24

The Temple of Concord was transformed into a Christian religious building in the 7th century AD and dedicated to Saints Peter and Paul. This conversion of the temple into a church involved an evident transformation of the structure of the building to adapt it to the requirements of the new cult. On the other hand, this permitted the building's substantial conservation thanks to the work of restoration and upkeep to which it was subjected. This has enabled it to survive the injuries of time and to be preserved down to our own day. In the 18th century it was restored to its original form, and took on the appearance we can now admire today.

Here and following pages, more delightful images of the Temple of Concordia, a splendid example of Doric architecture in Sicily.

Erected on a restricted strip of flat ground on the crest of the hill of the Temples, the Temple of Concord occupies a majestic position above the fortifications which enclosed ancient Akragas from this side.On the flat esplanade in front of the temple the traces of Byzantine-Christian tombs are visible.Not far from the road that skirts the temple are the Early Christian cemetery and the so-called **Grotta di Frangipane**, a term designating a group of underground tombs with a typically circular plan.

Temple of Juno or Hera Lacinia

A complex of extraordinary beauty, it is situated in a spectacular position on the crest of the hill of the Temples. The views which it is possible to enjoy from this spot over the surrounding territory, the valley, the sea and the whole archaeological zone are magnificent. Below are the massive rock walls which support the temple and the fortifications, which in this stretch are naturally incorporated in the ridge of the escarpment thus offering a natural buttress to the western flank of the Temple of Juno. This stretch of the ancient ramparts was pierced by an ancient gateway (Gate II). The extraordinary remains of the temple itself preserve in large part intect the great podium on which it stands, approached by high steps built of squared blocks of stone, over which the colonnade of the north side of the sanctuary rises; the line of columns is still in large part intact. It is surmounted throughout its length by an architrave. Other fluted Doric columns, in part still intact and they too bearing the architrave on top, are placed along the temple's perimeter (this temple too was peripteral and hexastyle). The temple was erected in the mid-5th century BC, and was dedicated to Hera (Juno) to which the epithet Lacinia has been added due to a confusion with a similar temple at Crotone near Capo Lacinio. The structure of the building essentially recalls that of the Temple of Concord, to which it is slightly anterior in date.

This page, the Temple of Juno, dedicated to the daughter of Cronus and Rhea, wife of Jupiter and protectress of marriage.
The temple is situated on the highest point of the hill.

Right, a detail of the beautiful colonnade on the south-west side. In the foreground are steps added to the terraces at the base during the Roman period.

Following pages, scenic views of the Temple of Juno.

The views offered by these photos testify eloquently to the monumentality of the remains of the temple and especially to the uniqueness of its position.

They show in particular the defensive bastions which accompany the rocky crest and the siting of the temple on the highest point of the hill.

The effect of the columns silhouetted against the blue of the sky is majestic.

The aerial view on the facing page shows the peripteral and hexastyle plan of the temple and its raised position.

Here and following pages, more magnificent views of the Temple of Juno: after the Temple of Concordia, this is the best preserved in Agrigento.

The Ekklesiasterion and Oratory of Phalaris

We are in the archaeological zone located around the small hill of San Nicola, where the church of the same name and the Regional Archaeological Museum are situated.

In this area of the ancient city the residual traces of the chequerboard network of streets can still be identified. Here too we may find the remains of a temple and of the so-called **Ekklesiasterion**, a kind of open-air theatre built in the 3rd century BC, i.e. in the Hellenistic period; it is in large part hewn into the rock.

Its function was to provide an open-air venue for popular assemblies (as testified by its name which indicated the community of citizens). It therefore fulfilled an eminently civic function and constituted, as it were, the theatre of political debate and public consultations (*Comitia*).

To one side of it rose the massive structure of the **Oratory of Phalaris** a sacred building later in date than the Ekklesiasterion and belonging to the 1st century BC. It was long thought to be the tomb of an illustrious man, but it is in fact a small sanctuary dedicated to the gods, resting on a high rectangular basement. At one time it was preceded by a pronaos, which was swept away due to the alterations to which the monument was subjected in the Middle Ages, when it was converted into a Christian chapel and probably linked to the nearby church of San Nicola.

It was from its new function that its name of Oratory derives.

The name of Phalaris, on the other hand, recalls the first of the tyrants of ancient Akragas.

A lovely view of the hall where assemblies of the populace were held, and of the Phalaris Oratory, originally dedicated to ancient divinities and transformed into a Christian chapel during the middle ages.

Following pages – a wonderful panorama over the Valley of the Temples.

The Doric temple in Sicily

The many temples that dot the landscape of Sicily and give the island what we might call a "Greek look," are in absolute dominated by the Doric style. The only known exception, not only in Sicily but indeed in the entire Greek west, is a great Ionic temple in Syracuse. The few remains that have come down to us are partially visible in the subterranean area of the modern portion of the Palazzo Municipale of Syracuse. Ionic elements are nevertheless sometimes to be seen in eminently Doric structures, like the small 4th century BC temple at Megara Hyblaea and the archaic temple, probably dedicated to Aphrodite, at Akrai (Palazzolo Acreide).

The Doric order developed on the Greek mainland in the 7th and 6th centuries BC, is characterized above all by the absence of a column base; the columns rest directly on the upper step (**stylobate**) of the aboveground base of the temple (**crepidoma**).

The Doric column generally has from 16 to 20 flutes and terminates in a simple capital made up of a bowl-shaped **echinus** and a square **abacus**. The columns support the entablature: a smooth architrave with above it a **frieze**, composed of panels decorated with reliefs (**metopes**) alternating with rectangular slabs with vertical grooves (**triglyphs**). The two short sides of the temple are topped by a triangular **pediment** with **acroteria** at the corners; the **cornice** of the pediment delineates the **tympanum**, which is usually decorated in relief.

The central element of the temple is the rectangular cella or **naos**, which usually receives light only from the door; the statue of the deity stood in the **adyton** in the interior of the naos. When the cella is surrounded on all sides by columns, the temple is said to be **peripteral**; if the colonnade is double, the temple is **dipteral**.

If the building has columns only on the facade between the extensions of the longitudinal walls of the cella — which thus create a vestibule or **pronaos** — it is said to be "**in antis**" (the pronaos structure, when repeated on the rear of building, is called an **opisthodomos**). If the pronaos is preceded by a colonnade, the temple is said to be **prostyle**. The number of columns on the short side is usually six; hence the term **hexastyle**.

Reconstruction of a Doric-style temple.

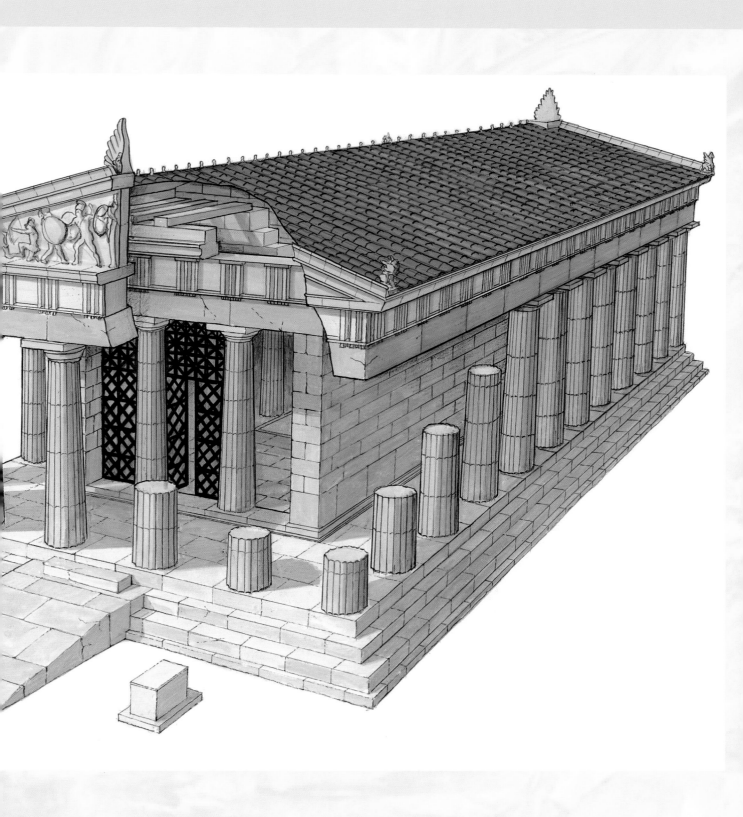

Regional Archaeological Museum

The Regional Archaeological Museum has been installed within the archaeological zone of Agrigento. It occupies the rooms of the former Monastery of San Nicola and also a large building of recent construction, inaugurated in 1967. It is situated on the edge of the area occupied by the Ekklesiasterion and the Oratory of Phalaris. Thanks to the wealth of the materials collected, their historical and artistic importance, and the civilizations to which they bear witness, the Museum constitutes one of the most interesting and comprehensive museum complexes not only in Sicily but in Italy as a whole. The precious collection is divided into two major sections according to the provenance of the finds: the first is strictly confined to the finds made in the Valley of the Temples and in the territory immediately surrounding the city of Agrigento; the second is devoted to all the materials recovered from the province of Agrigento and to part of those from neighboring Caltanisetta. As regards the periods and civilizations represented here, they range from the prehistoric period, and hence from finds dating back to the remote Palaeolithic, to Mycenean, Greek and Hellenistic times, and lastly to the whole of the Roman period, thus encompassing the whole succession of foreign occupations in Sicilian territory during antiquity. The materials and artefacts gathered together in the museum are of various kind: they range from objects of everyday use, such as the primitive pointed stone tools and weapons of the Palaeolithic to the first coarse pottery vessels; to the vast collection of variously decorated vases, depending on the periods and cultures to which they belong; to the wonderful works of sculpture found in the territory; to the whole rich repertory of votive deposits found in the numerous sanctuaries and shrines of the zone and the funerary material from the cemeteries. Last but not least of the museum's holdings are the various architectural and decorative fragments from the temples of Agrigento. They include numerous inscriptions and, especially, the mighty Telamon from the Temple of Zeus, which has been reconstructed here to ensure its better conservation and also to enable it to be appreciated in all its colossal proportions and beauty. The numismatic collection is also very rich and of the greatest interest. The Archaeological Museum is also furnished with models, plans, reconstructions and photos which play an effective educational role and help the visitor to gain a better knowledge of the territory. The collection as a whole is one that testifies to the historical, political, economic and artistic importance attained by ancient Akragas through the centuries.

General view of the lovely church of San Nicola. The monastery houses part of the Museo Archeologico Regionale (Regional Archaeological Museum).

The head of a Telamon from the Temple of Jupiter.

Right, head of a man sculpted in marble (Hercules?).

Fragment of Roman mosaic.

A splendid marble torso dated 5th century B.C.

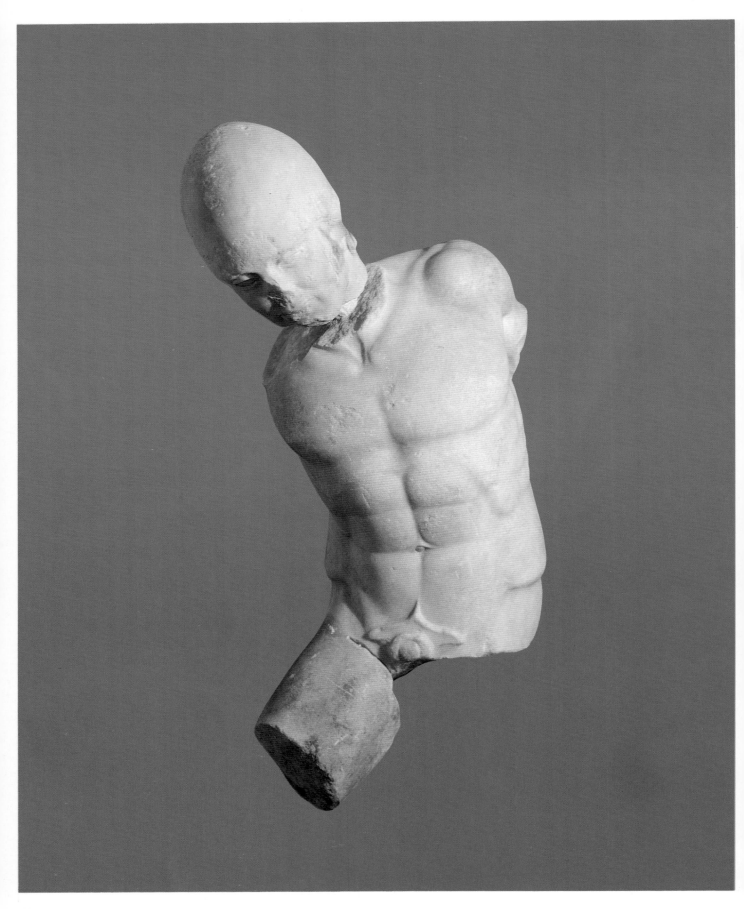

GREEK WARRIOR: The statue, in part mutilated, represents a warrior who has sunk to the ground in combat and is supporting himself on one knee, but continues to defend himself. The statue is datable to 480 BC and hence belongs to the archaic period of Greek sculpture. In spite of the semi-recumbent position of the warrior, it is possible to identify in the statue the canons of ancient Greek art which sought to achieve compositional balance in their works through the so-called position of chiasm (i.e. the forward projection of the left arm and shoulder, which is always matched by the backward projection of the right leg, and vice versa).

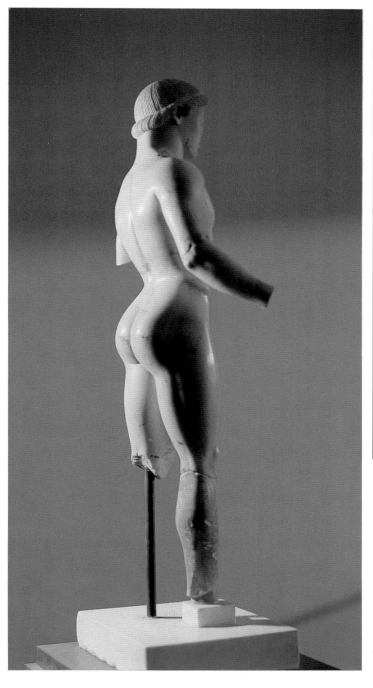

EPHEBE: This is one of the most famous statues of antiquity and also one of the most precious pieces in the museum. It is a Greek sculpture dating to the 5th century BC, and hence to the archaic phase of Greek art. The figure, in an erect position, presents in a subtle and barely accentuated way the position of chiasm and embodies the canons of beauty and harmony peculiar to ancient art, which pursued its search for perfection especially through the reproduction of the features of the human body.

Above, a room in the Archaeological Museum where one of the Telamons from the Temple of Jupiter is displayed.

Below, another room in the museum where a fine collection of artefacts from Agrigento and other nearby areas are exhibited.

Right, a beautiful red figure Attic vase.

 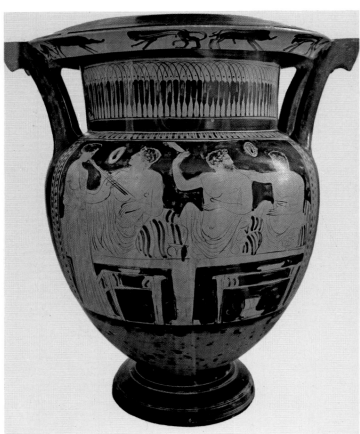

Two vases from the fine collection housed in Room III of the museum, which contains an excellent range of ceramic items dating from the 5th to 3rd century B.C. including typical examples of Attic and Hellenic-italianate vases.

Below, the remains of a Roman sarcophagus.

Above, the Phaedra sarcophagus, a sophisticated and elegant Roman piece, dated 2nd century A.D., inspired by similar earlier Greek sarcophagi. The myth of Phaedra and Hippolytus is portrayed on the sides: Hippolytus receives a declaration of love from Phaedra before going out to hunt; Phaedra's dismay when her love is refused; the boar hunt; Hippolytus flung from his chariot.

Below, a late-Roman sarcophagus.

53

Church of San Nicola

The church of San Nicola is situated in the archaeological zone of the Hellenistic and Roman quarter.

The building has a particular and quite distinctive shape. Erected by using the material of which the zone was abundantly supplied, it was probably begun by the Normans (there is mention of a pre-existing palace of Phalaris) and completed by the Cistercians in the early 13th century, though some modest alterations are attributable to subsequent Franciscan restorations.

In essence, the church is Romanesque in form, but the fine portal and other stylistic features introduce clear gothic motifs.

The facade of the church is well-characterized: at once simple and ponderous.

A handsome portal, framed by serried rows of elegant gothic arches, is placed between two massive projecting wings.

The whole lower part of the facade is emphasized by a pronounced cornice.

The upper part is formed by a ridged pediment and essentially unadorned. Two bas-relief panels are built into the upper part of the

Three views of the church.

two massive piers.

Inside the church consists of a single nave and four chapels placed on one side only. The surfaces are articulated by a cornice and, on the end wall, by niches, a large central arch, and a

blind loggia containing 16th century frescoes.

Particularly interesting, and of great scenic appeal, are the small 14th century **Cloisters** which are surrounded by a series of gothic arcades in tufa, with a well-head placed at the centre.

Hellenistic-Roman quarter

The archaeological discovery of this zone occurred in relatively recent times. A series of studies and field-surveys were conducted in the mid-century, aimed at the more precise delimitation of the urban area which could be identified with ancient Agrigento, also on the basis of the previous surveys. This led in turn to a systematic campaign of excavations, which uncovered a huge urban area covering over 10,000 square metres and known as the Hellenistic-Roman quarter.

Aerial view of the Hellenistic-Roman area.

It dates as a whole to the 4th century BC (occupying entirely an area which had already been urbanized during previous centuries) and testifies unequivocally to the importance attached to Akragas during those years and to the significant economic and political, as well as territorial, development of which it was the protagonist.

The plan of the quarter forms a regular chequerboard. The buildings were arranged along parallel and rectilinear streets, intersected by an equal number of straight roads running at right angles to them. The main thoroughfares of the city, i.e. the so-called *decumani*, led to an equal number of **Gates**. Together they formed the basic infrastructure of the quarter. The buildings in the quarter were developed over a long period, and hence provide a panorama of the various types of Greek-Hellenistic and Roman houses. Apart from houses, villas and warehouses, it is possible to recognise a number of other structural types, such as *tabernae* (taverns), wells and especially a well-developed water-supply system which, thanks to an efficient network of terracotta pipes, was also able to serve private houses.

Of particular interest are the remains of some villas. Apart from some rather ruined wall structures, they are notable for their fine mosaic and mural decorations, some of them of exquisite workmanship. Almost all represent geometric or animal and plant motifs.

Partial view of the area and the buildings standing along the axis of the main roads.

Right, the colonnade of an arisocratic villa with part of the decorated horizontal beam still preserved.

COPPIA DI TABERNAE

Above, the remains of a nobleman's residence with the colonnade of the peristyle still standing, showing traces of the decorative plasterwork; beside, one of the two taverns in the area, showing the counter with holes where the wine-jars were inserted. Below, a view of the Hellenic-Roman area.

Right, the road cut into the rock, an integral part of the fortification system of the ancient Sicilian city.

The street hewn in the rock

THE DEFENSIVE SYSTEM OF AKRAGAS: THE GATES AND WALLS OF THE ANCIENT CITY:

The street hewn in the rock is undoubtedly an archaeological find of rare suggestion because, like other even more important archaeological finds in ancient Akragas, it provides some indication of the extraordinary fortifications which delimited the city and its acropolis. It also bears witness to the impressive engineering works involved in developing this defensive system and overcoming the resistence of the rock and the difficulties of the terrain. The street (situated in the vicinity of Gate II), hewn into the living rock, still bears the ruts of the waggons which ascended the hill with their merchandise and passengers and which, by traversing the gates in the walls and skirting the bastions, linked the upper part of Akragas with the roads below leading down to the coast. It thus forms an integral part of the system of fortifications of the ancient Sicilian city. Surrounding the Acropolis or Rupe Atenea, i. e. the upper part of the city, it exploited the natural ruggedness of the plateau, using natural features to supplement or buttress its defensive works. The system followed the line of the escarpment of the plateau, comprising a succession of curtains of wall, bastions and gates which connected the city with the Valley of the Temples and descended to the river Akragas below. So far 9 gates in the circuit of walls have been identified by the excavations; part of them have been excavated, part only identified on the ground. The eastern side of the defensive system was pierced by Gates I and II (the latter pointing towards Gela, whose name it also takes). These are solid in structure and situated in proximity of the Acropolis and the stretch of massive fortifications known as "tenaille fortifications", in which the bastions project outwards in two converging spurs to form a kind of pincers, to block the influx of hostile forces. On the southern side Gate III, Gate IV and Gate V led through the walls. The second of these was also known as the Golden Gate (it was the most important in the city), and was situated close to the Temple of Hercules. The third was the closest to the Temple of Zeus. In the stretch of the fortification in the vicinity of Gate III, various tombs of the Christian period have been found, hewn into the living rock; they date to the 3rd and 4th century AD. The other gates (Gates VI, VII, VIII and IX) pierced the walls on the western side.

Rock sanctuary of Demeter

The rock sanctuary of Demeter, which is reached by a precipitous flight of steps cut into the rock, is situated outside the ancient circuit of walls, and this suggests that its construction preceded it. Discovered in 1926, and revealed in its entirety a few years later, it is thought to date to the late 7th century BC and hence to represent the most ancient sanctuary of Agrigento, antedating the foundation of the Greek city itself. Perhaps dedicated to the cult of Demeter, the Sanctuary consists of two large galleries hewn into the rock and preceded by a rectangular vestibule. Outside there is a system of intercommunicating basins, they too hollowed into the rock, evidently attesting to the ancient cult of water. Numerous statuettes and busts of Demeter and Kore, vases and oil-lamps have been found in the walls of the galleries.

Three beautiful views of the sanctuary.

Church of San Biagio

This church was built in the Norman period over the ruins of a pre-existing Greek temple, probably dedicated to the goddesses Demeter and Kore. Of this temple, dating to roughly the years 480-470 BC, the foundations and the bases of the pronaos, still recognisable behind the apse of the church, remain. Two circular altars can also be distinguished behind the apse, but further uphill from the church.

Temple of Vulcan

Built on the extreme edge of the rocky escarpment rising over the valley of the river Hypsas in the vicinity of the Temple of the Dioscuri and the Sanctuary of the Chthonian Deities, the Temple of Vulcan was probably the last sacred building to be built on the plateau of Akragas. It dates to the 5th century BC. A sacred shrine existed previously on the same site. It was later incorporated into the temple and comprised in the cella dedicated to the god. Like other sacred buildings at Akragas, this temple too is peripteral and hexastyle.

A large part of its foundations survive; high steps lead up to the stone-built podium. Two fluted and in part mutilated columns also survive.

Above, remains of the Greek temple that pre-existed the church of San Biagio. Below, the apse of the church.

Opposite, the remains of the Temple of Vulcan.

The Cathedral

The Cathedral of Agrigento draws the visitor's attention by its complex and austere appearance and by the composite articulation of its structural parts, attesting to the various periods and phases in its construction. It stands on the acropolis of Agrigento, more or less on the site on which, according to tradition, a temple dedicated to Zeus formerly stood. The Cathedral is dedicated to St. Gerlando, whose reliquary is housed in a special urn in the chapel dedicated to him. Though begun in the 11th century, the general appearance of the church today is that of its Norman-gothic reconstruction in the 13th and 14th century. The Cathedral was also remodelled in the 16th and 17th century. The styles that accompanied its construction are thus various and not easy to disentangle. It is however easy enough to identify the 17th century baroque remodelling in its facade and its high flight of stairs in front. The great bell-tower beside the church, which was never completed, dates by contrast to the 15th century. It presents, on the side overlooking the street, an elegant series of gothic windows and a graceful balcony in a pure gothic style.

Inside too, the Cathedral is characterized by the various styles and alterations to which it has been subjected through the centuries, although the arcades that divide the nave from the aisles have in part been restored to their original forms.

The decorations of the Cathedral are mainly attributable to the 17th century, including its fine coffered ceiling and the stuccoes that embellish the sanctuary.

The Chapel of St. Gerlando and the De Marinis Chapel are opened by elegant gothic arcades.

Various works of painting and sculpture can also be admired in the church: in particular, a fine panel of Guido Reni depicting the "Madonna and Child" is kept in the adjoining Sacristy.

The building is famous for its excellent acoustics.

The side of the belltower with a double order of single-light windows with particularly fine Gothic arches. Above these another magnificent single-light window with beautiful decorations opens onto a lovely balcony. In the upper section of the belltower, above a narrow cornice, two deeply arched windows open onto the bell chamber.

Left, a view of the cathedral.

Church and Monastery of Santo Spirito

Magnificent architectural complex situated in the historic centre of Agrigento, it was erected for the wife of Federico Chiaramonte.

It comprises the **Church of Santo Spirito** and the **Monastery**, both built from 1290 in the gothic style with Chiaramontan elements, and subsequently remodelled in various periods, especially in the 17th century.

The wonderful and distinctive facade of the church presents a handsome and elegant gothic portal, above which there is a gothic rose-window.

The three small bell- chambers on top date to the baroque period.

Inside the church is remarkable for its fine 17th century stucco decoration, attributable to Serpotta. The Monastery was assigned to the Cistercian order.

The building is complex but harmonious, and given great elegance by the series of fine gothic arcades with delicately decorated interspaces which articulate its surfaces, and by the exquisite details that decorate the structural elements of the cloister, such as the capitals of the colonnettes of the two-light mullioned windows or the arcades of the Chapter House and Cloisters.

The rooms of the Monastery, and in particular the former Refectory, now house the local Civic Library.

The façade of the church, with the Gothic doorway and rose window. Below, a series of magnificent doorways with Gothic arches.

Right a view of the cloister with the elegant doorway leading to the Gothic Room on the first floor.

Luigi Pirandello

An illustrious son of Sicily, Luigi Pirandello was born at Girgenti (Agrigento) in 1867. His works have left their mark on an entire epoch, and on the literature of the first half of this century, with their well-defined character and great originality.

Apart from novels and essays, he also wrote stage-plays. for which he is now best remembered. Among his most famous plays are "Six Personages in Search of an Author" and "Henry IV", which remain among the most significant achievements of the Italian theatre and have had a major influence on world literature. Pirandello was honored for his literary achievements.

He was not only nominated Academician of Italy, but also awarded the Nobel Prize for Literature in 1934.

His output is shot through by a dark vein of pessimism and the existential anguish which pervaded the whole period. Each man, for Pirandello, wears a mask in front of his fellowmen and society: a mask which he involuntarily ends up by resembling.

Appearance and reality thus become fused. Man seems to lose his own identity, in the search for a reality that eludes him.

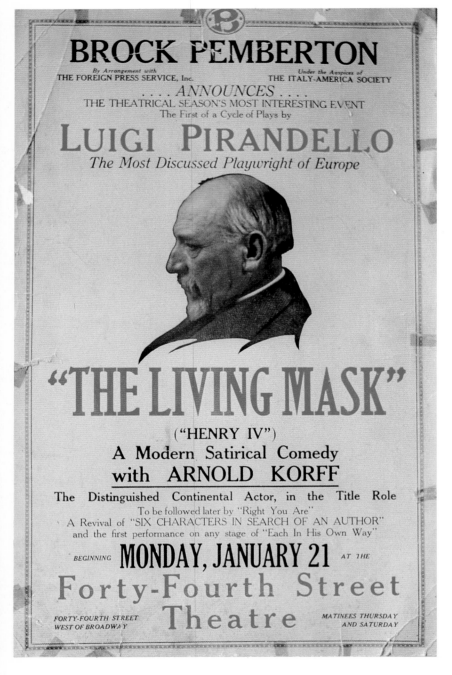

Two interior views of the house where Pirandello was born, with furniture and items of the period. The photographs on the walls record events in the life of the author. Now a national monument, numerous visitors come to the house.

*Three portraits of Luigi Pirandello:
a high school student (1885),
university student in Palermo
(1887) and in later life.*

*Centre and below, the house where
the writer was born and the solitary
pine tree where he is buried.*

MY LAST WILL AND TESTAMENT

*May my death be passed over in silence.
I pray to my friends, as to my enemies,
not to speak of me in the newspapers,
indeed not to mention me at all.
No announcements, no participation.
Once I am dead, do not dress me.
Wrap me naked in a sheet.
And no flower son the bed
and no lighted candles.
A hearse of the lowest class,
that of the poor. Naked.
Let no one accompany me,
neither relations, nor friends.
The hearse, the horse, the coachman and
that's all. Burn me. And let my body,
as soon as it is burnt, be left to disperse, because
I wish nothing, not even the ashes, to remain of me.
But if this is not possible, let the cinerary urn
be taken to Sicily and immured in
some rough stones in the countryside
 of Girgenti where I was born.*

Coast of Agrigento

The coast of Agrigento may be considered the shoreline comprised between the locality of Sciacca to the west and Licata to the east, and consists of a long succession of littorals to which the slopes of the hills to the rear descend.

The reduced area of seacoast facing the city consists of a series of small bays and cliffs dropping to the sea either more gently in sloping terraces, or more precipitously with imposing rocky promontories, on which ancient guard-towers can sometimes be glimpsed.

Water erosion has left its indelible mark on the coastline, creating fantastic rock architectures, with their extraordinary scenery of rugged cliffs, dark fissures and caves, or rock-walls dropping sheer to smooth sandy beaches.

In this magnificent setting, the colors of the sea and the sky only heighten the incomparable beauties of nature.

Some lovely views of the coast near Agrigento.

75

Porto Empedocle

maritime and industrial centre, it is the most important port of the south-western coast of Sicily. The original nucleus of the town was formed in the second half of the 18th century, at the behest of the bishop Ugo Gioeni; it was founded between the waterfront which offered a good natural landing- place and the slopes of Monte Crasto.

It owes its name to the famous philosopher of Agrigento, Empedocles.

In the vicinity of Punta Piccola, which is notable for its fine beach, may be found the remains of a building probably of the Roman period, with mosaic floors decorated with floral and geometric motifs. The harbour is dominated by a Fortress built by the Spaniards in 1584 and now converted into a prison.

The town's development was linked to the Port, which underwent a notable expansion in the early 1880s when the mining of sulphur began.

Today the port handles large volumes of imports and exports, and its considerable harbor facilities enable it to refuel ships in transit. It is also the point of embarkation for the islands of Linosa and Lampedusa. Porto Empedocle's tourist traffic is also constantly increasing.

Sunset over the sea and a view over the city.

Heraclea Minoa

This is an interesting archaeological zone situated on the southern coastal strip of Sicily between Sciacca and Licata, in the vicinity of Cape Bianco and the mouth of the river Platani. The territory in question has recently been declared protected, to safeguard the local flora and fauna.

The origin of Heraclea Minoa is almost certainly to be ascribed to Mycenaean civilization, over which was superimposed, in the 6th century BC, the Greek colonization promoted by Selinus (Selinunte).

Like many other Sicilian cities, it suffered the various political and social vicisssitudes of the region, beset by the ferocious rivalry first between the Greeks and the Carthaginians, and then between the Carthaginians and the Romans, in their respective bids to extend their dominion over the island and, especially, to ensure themselves of maritime and commercial hegemony. The excavations of the area have a relatively recent history. Only begun in the early years of the 20th century, they were pursued with greater commitment in the years of the mid-century. The remains uncovered and the studies conducted have revealed the town plan with stratifications attributable to various periods and civilizations, superimposed over each other in time. In addition the excavations have revealed some stretches of the circuit of walls which, with its system of towers and fortifications, ensured the city's defence. The archaeological remains now visible include a fine Theatre, various houses attributable in the main to Greek architecture of the Hellenistic period. The excavations have also uncovered an extensive area in the surrounding territory occupied by burial sites. It is from them that most of the grave goods, vases and various artefacts now displayed in the Antiquarium annexed to the archaeological area come. The small Museum also houses the pottery and household goods found in the Hellenistic houses excavated in the town itself. A section is also dedicated to the prehistoric weapons and artefacts found in the deeper strata of the terrain. These finds attest to the presence of man in the territory ever since the Stone Age.

The archaeological site at Heraclea Minoa, set amidst beautiful scenery.

Sciacca

A heavily populated little town in the lower Belice valley, Sciacca is spread out over a terrace which slopes gradually down to the south-eastern coastal strip of Sicily between the Belice and Plani rivers. It is one of the best known resorts in the island, as it was in the past, when it was appreciated as a spa and its waters utilized for therapeutic purposes. The Romans gave it the name of Thermae Selinuntinae, thus indicating both the presence of thermal waters, and its dependence on the neighboring and more important Selinunte.

The Arab domination, which was extended to this area from the 9th century (it is to this period that the place-name Sciacca dates), turned the town into a commercial centre of major importance and conferred on it a large part of the urban layout which still characterizes the historic town centre, and over which the medieval town plan was in large part superimposed.

The current town plan, however, is preponderantly that determined in the 16th and 17th centuries when the whole town was surrounded by an imposing circuit of walls and the centre was subjected to a total reorganization, with the present Piazza del Popolo forming its centre of gravity. Much of Sciacca thus presents an urban fabric of baroque type, as is plain in many of the buildings that still embellish it today, or in the way that the various older palaces and churches are decorated. This goes for example for the Cathedral, which was erected in the medieval period (as its three fine surviving Norman apses attest), but which was remodelled in the mid-17th century, both in plan and in decoration (the work of Gagini). The same goes too for the handsome church of Santa Margherita with its magnificent portal in the gothic- Renaissance style realized by the architect Laurana and De Bonitate, subsequently transformed in its structure and decorated with 17th century stuccoes.

A delightful view of the city th its colourful harbour.

PALAZZO STERIPINTO

This is a strikingly original palace situated close to the Corso Vittorio Emanuele. What is particularly striking about it is the original rustication of its facade; this takes the form of a diamond-pointed stone facing, which confers on the building a pronounced contrast between light and shade. The severity of the wall surfaces was then relieved by the elegant two-light mullioned windows, the fine Renaissance portal and the delicate crenellated rooftop.

The palace was built in the early years of the 16th century; in style it represents a fusion between local idiom and a Catalan influence.

Above left, the Sanctuary of
San Calogero and, right,
Palazzo Steripinto.
Left, a panoramic view of Sciacca.

CAMMORDINO CLIFF AND GROTTO

This is the name of the soaring cliff which forms part of the littoral of Sciacca and is situated right below the thermal buildings.

THE BATHS

The Baths comprise a huge complex of various facilities which exploit the therapeutic properties of the water. The Selinuntine Baths (they still retain the ancient name of the town of Sciacca) are now divided into various sectors, each specialized in the treatment of the various rheumatic, uro-genital or respiratory illnesses, and also skin disorders. It is interesting to note that all the water used in these various establishments comes from Monte San Calogero. A visit to this mountain will enable us to discover some interesting karst phenomena (i.e. the underground streams, gorges and caves characteristic of limestone areas), and more especially the so-called "baths of San Calogero", which are a source of vapor emitted by the caves below. Fossil material has been found in the caves of the mountain and now preserved in the nearby Antiquarium. This material shows that the caves were inhabited from prehistoric times, and that the vapors emanated by them were exploited from antiquity onwards.

CASTELLO DEI LUNA

This is a medieval castle dating to the final years of the 14th century, of which only the outer walls and massive tower remain. It takes its name from the noble family that inhabited it from the 15th century on.

Above, the impressive cliff below the spa resort; below, the ruins of the Castello dei Luna (Luna Castle).

Licata

Licata is spread out between the mouth of the river Salso and the slopes of the hill known as "La Montagna". It boasts of very ancient origins, as attested by the finds brought to light in the surrounding archaeological area; they attest to the presence of man in the area since prehistoric times. Inhabited first by the Greeks and then by the Romans, it continued to prosper also under the Byzantines (of whom several rock churches remain), and especially in the medieval period. It was then that much of its surviving town plan was developed within a robust circuit of walls, gravitating round two castles which have since disappeared.

From antiquity onwards Licata has played the role of a thriving agricultural and commercial centre, also favored by its well-equipped harbour, developed round a quiet natural landing place.

This enabled Licata to enjoy a strong economic expansion and, simultaneously, a significant urban and building development which was particularly intense in the 17th and 18th centuries, as attested by the numerous palaces and monuments that still embellish the town today.

A romantic sunset over the sea and, right, a panorama of the city.

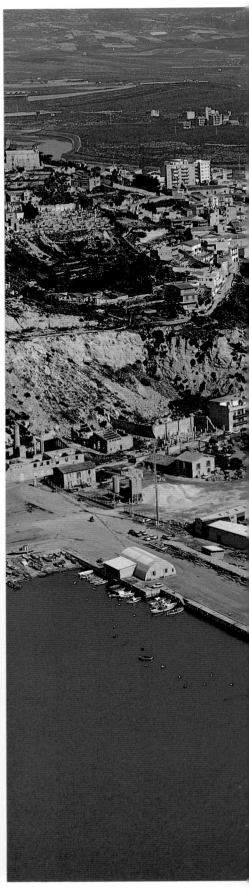

Palma di Montechiaro

This populous town is situated on the slopes of Monte Pozzillo, along the coastal strip which stretches east from Agrigento to Licata and Gela. Palma di Montechiaro's name is inseparably linked with the Tomasi di Lampedusa family, ancestors of the author of "The Leopard", who had their dukedom here; they inherited it from that of the De Caro.

The town's name derives from the palm that represented the heraldic emblem of the De Caro family and from the feud of the Montechiaro which formed an integral part of the territory together with the neighboring castle of the Chiaramonte.

The town arose in the 17th century, under the patronage of two noble families (De Caro and Tomasi), exploiting the scenic position of the site, its accessibility to the main roads of the island and also the resources of the territory.

The town plan reveals a precise design based on a regular gridiron of streets which have their fulcrum in the central Piazza Provenzani. Developed along these orthogonally laid out streets, the town was speedily embellished by its various 17th century monumental buildings. Among the many palaces and churches we may mention in particular the **Church of the Holy Rosary** (begun in 1637, it was the first building in the town), the **Benedictine Monastery** and especially: **the Mother Church of St. Mary of the Rosary.**

THE MOTHER CHURCH OF ST. MARY OF THE ROSARY

Built in the second half of the 17th century, it was based on a design by Angelo Italia. Particularly striking is its facade, which overlooks the Piazza di Santa Rosalia, on top of a wide flight of stairs. Two identical belfries enclose a two-storey loggia, articulated by deep windows and doors and twinned columns.

CASTLE OF MONTECHIARO

It was the original nucleus of the Montechiaro feud. Built in the late 14th century on the summit of the hill which dominates the whole coastline, perhaps at the behest of Federico III of Chiaramonte, its central structure, and part of the lateral wings and bastions, are still preserved.

Above, the Church of Santa Maria del Rosario stands on Piazza Santa Rosalia, at the top of a wide stairway.

Below and next page, the ruins of the Montechiaro Castle.

Island of Linosa

Linosa, the ancient "Algusa", forms part with Lampedusa and Lampione of the Pelagian Islands, situated in the province of Agrigento. Lying in the centre of the Mediterranean, actually closer to the coasts of North Africa than to those of Sicily, Linosa is a small oasis of tranquillity where nature is endowed with a wild beauty and the temperate climate offers an agreeable stay in any period of the year.

The island, its terrain dotted with gleaming white houses, and its people known for the cordiality of their welcome, is a favorite haunt of scuba divers, thanks to the exceptionally fish-rich waters of its seas.

It lies 42 km from Lampedusa. It is roughly square in shape and covers an area of 5.43 sq. km.

Already inhabited by the Romans and by the Arabs, Linosa was colonized by order of Ferdinand II in 1845. It is now inhabited permanently by 500 people, who are mainly engaged in farming and fishing.

Volcanic in origin, Linosa consists of basalt rocks, over which are superimposed very black deposits of lava, tufa and ash. The island emrged from the sea in the early Quaternary period.

A tranquil corner of the island of Linosa and, below, an aerial view.

Next page, another aerial view and, below, a lovely view from the sea.

Island of Lampedusa

Lampedusa, the "Lopadusa" of the Latins, is the largest and the most important of the Pelagian Islands. Situated just 113 Km from the coasts of Tunisia, but just over 200 Km from Sicily, Lampedusa is set in the "African Sea" and feels its influences, especially on its climate which it mild and constant throughout the year. Its northern coasts, jagged and dropping sheer to the sea, offer incomparable natural beauties, with a succession of little bays and caves, whose waters are a real paradise for scuba divers. Here abound groupers, hidden away in their lairs amid the emerald-green submarine grottoes, giltheads, umbras, mullets, and white bream.

On the less rocky and precipitous south-eastern side, the coasts slope down gently to the sea, and here a number of beaches of uncontaminated white velvety sand open up.

Traces have been found on the island of its ancient Phoenician, Greek, Roman and Arab inhabitants, but it was only in the mid-19th century that any real colonization of the island began, promoted by Ferdinand of Bourbon.

Equipped with a good port, Lampedusa is also provided with an airport which provides daily connections with Trapani and Palermo.

The permanent activities of the population are fishing for sponges which are exported throughout the whole world, and the fish-preserving industry, which comprises a number of establishments.

Today Lampedusa has been opened up for tourism and has begun to develop suitable facilities and infrastructures for this purpose.

A must for any visitor who wants to appreciate the natural environment to the full is a trip by boat round the island. By circumnavigating the island it is possible to admire the coastline in all its beauty. It is a succession of ever-varying views: of grottoes whose waters assume the dazzling colors of emerald green and peacock blue; of rocks emerging from the spume of the waves; of gentle little bays sheltering beaches of the finest sand; of picturesque corners bathed in silence.

The Scoglio del Faraglione emersed in crystal clear water, and the famous Spiaggia dei Conigli (Rabbit Beach).

*Cala Pisana, a picturesque bay that provides a natural
shelter for boats.*

Below, a beautiful part of the coast.

*Following pages, an incomparable view of the rugged cliffs
as they drop to the sea, seen from the edge of Albero del Sole.*

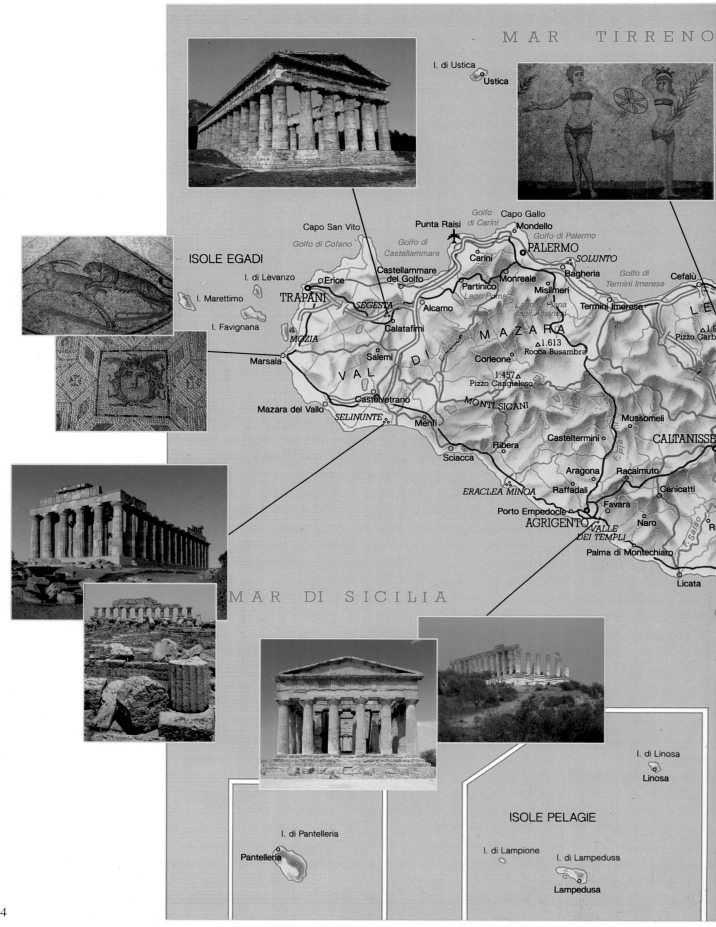

MAR TIRRENO

I. di Ustica
Ustica

ISOLE EGADI

I. di Levanzo

I. Marettimo

I. Favignana

Erice

TRAPANI

MOZIA

Marsala

Capo San Vito

Golfo di Cofano

Golfo di Castellammare

SEGESTA

Castellammare del Golfo

Calatafimi

Salemi

VAL DI

Punta Raisi

Golfo di Carini

Carini

Alcamo

Partinico

Lago Poma

Capo Gallo

Mondello

PALERMO

Monreale

Misilmeri

Lago di Piana degli Albanesi

MAZARA

Golfo di Palermo

SOLUNTO

Bagheria

Termini Imerese

Golfo di Termini Imerese

Cefalù

LE

Pizzo Carb

△1.6

Corleone

△1.613
Rocca Busambra

1.457△
Pizzo Cangialoso

MONTI SICANI

Castelvetrano

Mazara del Vallo

SELINUNTE

Menfi

Sciacca

Ribera

Mussomeli

Casteltermini

CALTANISSE

ERACLEA MINOA

Aragona

Raffadali

Porto Empedocle

AGRIGENTO

VALLE DEI TEMPLI

Racalmuto

Favara

Naro

Canicatti

Ri

Palma di Montechiaro

Licata

MAR DI SICILIA

I. di Linosa

Linosa

ISOLE PELAGIE

I. di Pantelleria

Pantelleria

I. di Lampione

I. di Lampedusa

Lampedusa

94

ISOLE EOLIE O LIPARI

I. Stromboli
I. Filicudi
I. Salina
I. Panarea
I. Alicudi
I. Lipari
Lipari
I. Vulcano

Capo Peloro
Capo Milazzo
Golfo di Milazzo
Golfo di Patti
Milazzo
TINDARI
Sant'Agata di Militello
Patti
Barcellona
Pozzo di Gotto
MESSINA
REGGIO DI CALABRIA
Stretto di Messina

VAL DEMONE
MONTI NEBRODI
△1.847
Monte Soro
MONTI PELORITANI
Gole d'Alcantara
Lago dell'Ancipa
Randazzo
Taormina
Giardini Naxos
Nicosia
Troina
Bronte
△2.414
Monte Pizzillo
△3.323
Monte Etna
Riposto
Giarre
Leonforte
Lago di Pozzillo
Adrano
Biancavilla
Belpasso
Acireale
Aci Trezza
Aci Castello
ENNA
Paternò
Misterbianco
Dittaino
CATANIA
Valguarnera Caropepe
Aidone
MORGANTINA
Golfo di Catania
Piazza Armerina
ROMANA DEL CASALE
Militello in Val di Catania
Capo Campolato
Caltagirone
Lentini
MAR IONIO
Grammichele
Francofonte
Augusta
MEGARA HIBLAEA
Golfo di Augusta
Niscemi
MONTI IBLEI
Floridia
DI GELA
NOTO
Palazzolo Acreide
SIRACUSA
Vittoria
RAGUSA
Capo Murro di Porco
Comiso
Noto
Avola
CAMARINA
Modica
Rosolini
Golfo di Noto
Scicli
Ispica
Pachino
Pozzallo
Capo Passero
MAR MEDITERRANEO

INDEX

© Copyright by CASA EDITRICE PERSEUS collection PLURIGRAF
Published and printed by Centro Stampa Editoriale, Sesto Fiorentino, (Fi).

The drawing on pp. 44-45 is by Stefano Benini. *The map on pp. 94-95 was made by* Alessandra Martini.
The photographs belong to the archive of Casa Editrice Plurigraf *and the archive of* Casa Editrice Bonechi.
The aerial photographs are authorised by S.M.A., *concession no. 506 and no. 850-86,
and were taken by* Ditta Ala Agricola S.r.l. - Bologna *and* I-BUGA.

Drawings of the cover: Sauro Giampaia

The publisher apologizes for any omissions and is willing to make amends with the formal recognition of rightful authors or owners.

ISBN 978-88-7551-027-5